T0324291

Autobiography of So-and-so:
Poems in Prose

Maurice Kilwein Guevara

New Issues Poetry & Prose

A Green Rose Book
Selected by William Olsen

New Issues Poetry & Prose
The College of Arts and Sciences
Western Michigan University
Kalamazoo, MI 49008

Copyright © 2001 by Maurice Kilwein Guevara. All rights reserved.
Printed in the United States of America

First Edition, 2001

ISBN: 0-932826-16-4 (paperbound)

Library of Congress Cataloging-in-Publication Data:
Kilwein Guevara, Maurice
Autobiography of So-and-So: Poems in Prose/Maurice Kilwein Guevara
Library of Congress Catalog Card Number (00-132575)

Art Direction: Tricia Hennessy
Design: Runako Simmons
Production: Paul Sizer
                  The Design Center, Department of Art
                  College of Fine Arts
                  Western Michigan University
Printing: Courier Corporation

Autobiography of So-and-so: Poems in Prose

Maurice Kilwein Guevara

New Issues

WESTERN MICHIGAN UNIVERSITY

Also by Maurice Kilwein Guevara

Postmortem
Poems of the River Spirit

for Don, Betty, Diego & Andrés

Contents

Return

Fast Forward

Afterlife

. . . I returned to this forgotten village, trying to put the broken mirror of memory back together from so many scattered shards.
—Gabriel Garcia Marquez

Autobiography of So-and-so: Poems in Prose

Self-Portrait

It looks, at first, like a wall of blue sky, some cumulonimbus threatening to build up on the side by the fire exit. You need to walk to the other part of the canvas and get down on your knees and there I am by the floor: the size of a railroad spike. I'm naked, head shaved to the bone, and the bead of water that fell a minute ago from the ceiling magnifies by three times the point at which my feet are crossed. Only now is it possible to tell where the errant vein disappears into the ankle. The other sound, beside the tinnitus of air conditioning, is the unseen pounding from a forge.

A baby anaconda cords my neck like an emerald helix. These moth wings are spread like a dark bell in the city; my eyes are about to open. By chance, the long molecule of a pheromone has just caught on a lash.

History Before Me

Reader of This Page

I had a dream in my mother's womb three days before I was born.

I remember I was called Andrés Cuevas and I had a different mother whose eyes were lizardgreen and who lit candles and spoke softly of how cool the breeze would be in the new year. I had many fathers in the dream; each came into my world alone with long black hair, a harelip, and twelve fingers like me. Each taught me something of wood: One walked along the coast and pointed out to me the different groves of trees; one showed me how to shape branches with fire; one had precise knowledge of metals and whetstones, while another made tiny crosses with twigs and tied them in my hair. Time passed in the dream, and one by one my fathers died of lung soreness or jaundice or of staring at the face of God in the ocean. I built each his coffin and let him sail deep in the white hot sand. Then comes the part where I am burned alive on the second day of February, 1614.

I remember you, reader of this page, as I remember the soldiers in the dream leading us through the streets to the plaza of Cartagena de Indias—the carpenter, the sorcerer, the Portuguese, the Devil's gentleman, and the peddler. Screams, chants, official proclamations, music from a shawm: The Governor held high the banner of Santo Domingo and the wooden cross I made for you, a priest I have loved my whole life, who read the final sentence, sweating.

My Mother as a Young Woman

My mother lost her virginity to a book about swords and sand and oil lamps and treason. On page one-hundred-and-forty-three was the word *virginidad*. Virgo. Stars in the celestial equator.

So there was no word for the night she spent with Bolívar in 1819 under the large green leaves and yellow flowers in his small bed in the *quinta* in Bogotá. There was no word for the awkward way he touched her elbow again and again or how she smelled coffee on his tongue the moment he spoke of France and Rousseau.

After a few minutes, he was finished and fell asleep facing the wall. Maps lay in the corner by his boots. She thought she heard the cook still at work in the kitchen.

That night she dreamed of a small white bridge over a stream of blood out in the country.

El 9 de abril

In the first ring of the circus year 1948:
The great Gaitán is murdered on the ninth of April, while far
away, in India, Gandhi is swirling peacefully out of control.

My grandmother is running with her girls down the streets of
Bogotá, small white dresses flying in the air, storefront glass crashing
all around them.

Eyes closed, what is the English rhyme my mother tries to
remember from school that morning?

Hello Mr. Traffic Cop
I'm going to the candy shop
To buy a present
For my sister's birthday party . . . .

Her eyes open as three men in *ruanas* bless a priest with
gasoline and rum and set him on fire. He twirls across Avenida
Caracas, his arms out, like a believer being sucked into hell. And into
the revolving door of the Tequendama Hotel, Fidel Castro disappears.

Still my mother remembers a certain yellow rose, the crow of
sirens, the rage of bells. Black smoke pouring from the newspaper
building while snakes with two legs slide out of the mountains or
retreat into plush suites. Bricks and fists, and more splinters of glass
falling as if from an ice storm.

Iron shoes of a horse gallop into a blind alley.

In hospital morgues, the constant squeaking of wheels.

My grandmother pulls the two sisters forward by their long
black hair, their feet trailing off the ground for several blocks. In the
flying blur, my aunt sees Jesus Christ, with fair skin and a gold tooth,
selling lottery tickets and fire crackers from a burning streetcar.

The Altar Boy

At the exact moment my mother's feet left the ground, the altar boy sat at the edge of his bed, in another hemisphere, masturbating for the first time. It was spring elsewhere beyond the great coke furnaces of Pittsburgh. I wish I could say there was a riot of white blossoms on a tree outside his bedroom window or the pinging of birds. There was only dark sky like the bottom of a man's workboot. Then the long muscles of his thighs tensed: oh nervous joy.

The altar boy listened for a full minute for my grandmother's feet on the wooden stairs. They never came. She was outside in the tiny backyard shaking out sheets and diapers already speckled with soot. Bells were clanging.

My father dressed and hurried to evening Mass, holding the white gown in the air. From a distance it looked like two lovers running across the iron bridge, late for their own wedding.

Birth

Memorial Day

My father is singing in dialect over the grave of my great grandmother. The sun is setting. The country is in another war.

My mother is planting nasturtiums over Nonna's grave, her green skirt shorter than the grass. A northern shrike is piercing a songbird on a thorn of barbed wire. When the old veterans push the Catholic cemetery gates closed, brown bats start to ricochet in the violet-tangerine sky.

The twins' first memory is of silence and the slight trembling of semen.

Postpartum

These lips of my mother are sad. After the twins were born, she found Pittsburgh the saddest place in any galaxy. The dirty yellow streetcars rocking through the starry hills left her crying in her hands.

Scrubbing diapers with a cracked washboard in a galvanized bucket on the fire escape of their second floor apartment on filthy Coltart Street. *Cucarachas* everywhere. Taking the Siamese twins to doctor after doctor and no one wanting to do anything. No one speaking Spanish. No Trio Los Panchos on the radio singing:

> *Atiéndeme*
> *Quiero decirte algo*
> *Que quizás no esperes*
> *Doloroso tal vez*

No Bogotá. No *almojábanas* warm from the ovens on Monserrate. No *Nuestra Señora de Guadalupe* looking over her city with the great arms open like wings. No racket of horse carts, no street vendors selling roses, no old men in open cafés discussing the endless feud of politics. No mother, no sister, no brother. No Andes, only these little hills and August soot and the sulfurous smell from the mill down by the river. That long moan of a train in the night.

The twins were sleeping back-to-back in the used crib. She woke my father to tell him they had to move back to Colombia. I heard this story from the great granddaughter of a *cucaracha*. She said the two made love like tense wolves, the cheap curtains blowing and blowing in the blue window.

The Fifth of November

By morning Mass in Belencito, my mother claims, she knew I would be born before noon. Her friend Inés put her nose in my mother's scalp and disagreed. "When it's time the roots of your hair will smell like *guayaba*." The priest was lifting the silver chalice above his head. In that curved and polished metal, the acolyte who would become a famous painter saw the open legs of my mother at the exact moment her water broke. A fox was whimpering outside the church and everyone agrees it was very, very windy that morning. My birth certificate states I was born with a harelip at five minutes to noon.

My mother kept her white socks and black shoes on during labor. I remember the explosion of light, foreign as English or Spanish. To make this house, many of us were crushed under pillars of wood.

Christ have mercy. Lamb of God. *Ite Missa est.*

Búho, Búho

Cuando sientas la barriga
como de puntillas llena
mascá raíz de manzanilla
con hojas de yerbabuena
—curación boyacense

We're stopped on the road from Belencito to Bogotá. In the convex sphere of an owl I see my six-month-old body cramping and weak in my mother's arms. My brothers are asleep next to us in the back seat. It's April, the rainy season. Many days and nights of diarrhea and wailing and vomiting and insomnia. Not able to drink even a coffeespoon of boiled water. The old doctor in our village finally showing the palms of his hands and turning his head to one side, as if to say: "Take this baby to the city before it's too late. My magic is from another time."

The old, borrowed Dodge has broken down in the middle of the mountain. My mother moves her wrist into the moonlight. 11:55. A small man and my father are under the hood with tools. My mother is quietly singing *"Reloj"* while holding the tip of her ring finger above my lips to feel the breathing. I see a match lighting a cigarette in the eye of the fluttering owl. The small man gets back in the driver's seat, looks over his shoulder at the lullaby, turns the key.

It begins to rain.

The last thing I see is my young father slamming the heavy hood.

Mirror, Mirror

My twin brothers were conjoined at the elbows until the age of two and a half. When one walked forward, the other pedaled backwards. They learned to dance by watching two candy wrappers swirl in the wind. If one said, "Tree," the other whispered, "Root." My father cut the connective tissue with a fresh razor blade, one morning after breakfast, and the two cried wildly for a long time because they felt invisible, a torso of sky beside train tracks.

To this day each brother cannot fall asleep unless his back is against a wall.

What Appear to Be Sunflowers

Every night alone in the kitchen my father heard voices. . . .
shipwreck with fifty-three confirmed dead . . . c'est une idéologie . . .
a kind of slow motion photography . . . self-imposed exile in Ghana.
Again, the passing of William Edward Burghardt Du Bois . . . is the
plan for the systematic removal of thousands of French troops from
Indo-China . . . Es ging aus und ein . . . dijo el alcalde de Guayaquil
. . . President's pledge to put men on the moon by the end of the
decade . . . partly cloudy over much of Denmark and Norway on
Tuesday . . . Bahía de Cochinos . . . from Red China. It is as real as
the meat hanging in your corner butcher shop.

The dial of the green short-wave radio he bought in Bogotá
was large like the center of a sunflower. My father watched the
vertical light move eastward across the fish skeleton. Morse code
lulled him. What he really loved were those inlets of abstract sound
waves. He listened to that range, the slow movement of pitch from
bass to treble, until one night he heard the voices of dead merchant
marines. They were beginning to see the yellow rims of round objects
glowing in the muddy water.

With These Scissors

With these long, brass-plated scissors from Germany, my mother made the green booties with red trim, the taupe *camisitas*, the paneled diapers, the wool *ruanitas* hanging on me and my brothers like grey bells in the wind in those photographs of us at the airport in Bogotá on the day we all left Colombia. With these scissors my mother cut *huascas* into the huge, blackened pot when she made *ajiaco*. And as the sun set over the mountains orange and red in our bedroom window, she used the scissors to shape the shadow of a crane flying over the bars of the crib. I was the fish.

One morning she saw I had kicked the little, white blanket off during the night. I was still asleep. Two inches from my neck lay a scorpion, burgundy and unmoving.

In the blink of an eye she severed it, the tail from the thorax.

The Projects

In Hazelwood, Wiping the Oilcloth
for the Hundreth Time

Soot, soot, soot. So many times my *abuelita* said that word,
I thought it meant I love you.

My Father Half-Stoned in the Projects

"Our family is like India," he whispered to me and my twin brothers, as we sat outside our unit in the Glen Hazel Housing Project. My father was drinking beer after supper, exhaling pale tendrils of marijuana like a beast with seven eyes. His hair was as long as that night, and he'd begun to teach himself to play a tin whistle he found abandoned the season before in the green dumpster.

Two units away: Freddie, black with one leg and almost blind, was listening to Nellie King call the Pirates' doubleheader on his transistor radio.

It was now dark, and I could see the orange flame from the mill, flickering. My father walked a few yards away to piss in the open field. The moon was large. There were fireflies and mosquitoes and the sound of cheering.

He came back and sat again on the cement stoop. "There's a holy man on his knees somewhere in India. Naked. He's rolling a coconut on the side of a highway. The truckers occasionally stop and have tea with him. He'll do this for six more years, a kind of prayer to Vishnu."

He picked up his tin whistle, jazzed something that reminded me of blue morning glories on a wire fence: I put my head on the cool concrete and fell asleep to my brothers laughing.

Behind the Stove

In those days I could make myself as small as a seed:
I followed the anxious *cucaracha* so closely she thought I was
her moon shadow or lover. She was in search of a perfect place. She
loved to zip into the darkness of my father's box of books, she adored
the smell of Huxley and Dickinson and Piaget's red-wine dust jacket.
When my brothers were asleep, she slipped behind the stove and into
the walls where I saw mice and dust and rivers and coke furnaces and
the long glass coolers at the Allegheny County Morgue. The inner
walls of the Projects were endless: I saw barges with coal like
pyramids, I saw badgers and a dead black bear beside the road where
Saint Bernard of Clairvaux was singing and walking through the
snowfall. I saw my mother's father signing papers in Chile. I was
walking through a maze of grape vines with the purple fruit hanging
in clusters the shape of South America. I saw my other grandfather
dying of cancer under a sheet with his eyes closed and his dirty glasses
on. Or was I a yellow canary flying through a mine?

When the *cucaracha* stopped, I stopped. She tipped her thorax
toward the seam of a gas pipe. We laid a string of perfect eggs.

It was already dawn.

My Grandmother's White Cat

When fiber-optic, sky-blue hair became the fashion, my father began the monthly ritual of shaving his head. It was August, and we were still living in the Projects without a refrigerator. The sound of my mother fluttering through the rosaries in another room reminded me of the flies I'd learned to trap in mid-flight and bring to my ear.

"Vecchio finally died," my father said, bending to lace his old boots. "You want to come help me?"

My grandparents lived in a green-shingled house on the last street before the Jones & Laughlin coke furnaces, the Baltimore & Ohio switching yard, and the sliding banks of the Monongahela. The night was skunk-dark. The spade waited off to the side.

Before I could see it, I could smell the box on the porch.

We walked down the tight alley between the houses to get to the backyard where fireflies pushed through the heat like slow aircraft and tomato plants hung bandaged to iron poles. My father tore and chewed a creamy yellow flower from the garden.

After a few minutes of digging, he said, "Throw him in."

I lifted the cardboard box above my head, so I could watch the old white cat tumble down, a quarter moon in the pit of the sky.

TV

When Freddie went completely blind because of the diabetes, he sold his television set to us for five dollars. We had to take the 56C down Second Avenue to replace two of the tubes, and that cost us four more dollars. The TV was black and white, which meant that everything was in different shades of gray. A pink Cadillac was gray. The Projects where we lived were gray. Robin's cape was gray. White and Black people were gray. Blood on the clothes of Cambodian children was a dark gray like shadows.

Walter Cronkite said the Moon was gray. He showed a picture of the Sea of Tranquility. He said there were highlands yet to be explored. He said to solve the problem of hovering would require a precise rocket throttle.

The planet rising above the slope of the horizon is Earth and you are blue.

Party Line

Bright spots from the TV in the other room flash on the wall beside me like heat lightning. I lift up the receiver just to snoop: Old Zomock Neni is talking to someone who only clears her throat occasionally. Zomock Neni's English is like following, through wet snow, some invader across Little Plain. Her mouth is a brown and white barn falling in on itself. She's complaining about sugar ants, how they're marching already behind her sink. She sprays, no good. She lights spaghetti on fire to burn the bastards out of their caves. The throat clears.

Now I hear my grandmother's television in the front room. A trained voice like a pecking bird is saying the war may now have already spread, by underground channels and night bombings, to Laos and Cambodia.

My Uncle Julius

As a little boy in Pittsburgh Julius saw heat molecules sliding down the neck of a steelworker, at night, birthday candles of the mill, the galaxy of deep space inside a nipple. What could have prepared him, before Vietnam, for the wet charred hand of a child at the base of the scorched tree, by the Hue River, steam over dark plum landscape and the small white teeth?

The Halloween Party

In the tenth grade we moved out to a mining patch; by this time Jock Yablonski had already joined Jesus and Lincoln and I was a striker, filthy from head to cleats after a Friday practice.

It was windy and the road was muddy through the hills. Rusty, a senior and goalkeeper, was driving his orange truck fast and shifting more than he had to. There were fiery and yellow leaves on the arms of the trees and blowing in the ditches and making light shadows in the woods. It was sunset by the time we pulled up to the gray house, unleashed dogs barking and lunging at the truck.

There was a large cross in the ground made of bundled cornstalks. And a barrel full of water and apples on the porch and a Confederate flag draped over the cushions of an old glider. When Rusty knocked, a man came to the screen door with his face painted black and a rope around his neck. He invited us into the kitchen, filled with people, each in costume.

There was a huge pumpkin on the table, and I could see the flames of the candles burning through the wicked twist of the eyes. I heard fiddle music from another room. Adolf Hitler offered me a pipe full of "red bud." I inhaled too much and coughed a cloud of smoke. People laughed. Hitler said try again, and this time I held the smoke in my lungs for a long time. A scarecrow threw a log in the buck stove. Rusty gave me a jelly glass full of whiskey, and a person with a yellow wig and a tight red dress and a low voice said, "Hey, so-and-so, guess who I am? I'm Venus." A hooded monk pushed me back on the porch and shoved my head in the apple barrel until I thought I was going to drown. Hitler pulled the revolver out of his holster and pointed it at the monk and asked did he know skunk season just started.

The fiddle got louder as I climbed the stairs. I was afraid I was going to be sick on the bed full of coats until the music stopped. Somebody was unknotting my sweats and I felt a tongue on me in the darkness. Next I heard the violin in another room and Rusty's voice calling my name from downstairs.

By the time we got into the truck to leave, the monk had already set the windy arms of the cross on fire.

Grimm the Janitor

Grimm the janitor dressed in civilian clothes.

He had one arm that didn't work completely. It was withered some and scarred but it served Grimm as a rest for his mop. I helped him the summer I was seventeen scrub and wax the classrooms of the elementary school. The whole time I worked for him he said *yes* and *nope* and *warsh that* and *move it* and *poosh that there* and very little else except for the day there was a thunderstorm; then he talked nonstop for twenty-five minutes.

Grimm said: "Stay in school, boy."

Grimm said: "I ain't educated, see, but least I got eyes."

Grimm said: "Dragonflies skin the water like them helicopters in Vietnam."

Grimm said: "Don't nobody got to make you pray or pledge allegiance to nothing."

Grimm said: "I use this hand to hold the phone when I talk to the talk show man on the AM radio and eat my frozen dinner and drink my Iron City and tell him war is rich old men spilling out the blood of the young and poor."

Grimm said: "Same hand I use to steady my .22."

Grimm said: "Ever skin a rabbit in the sunshine?"

Grimm said: "One day the government come knocking on my door and says, boy, now you got to get in a plane and fly a whole day and get off and kill some people you can't even talk to. They said yunz shoot that grandma, she's a spy what lives down in the ground."

Grimm said: "Once I even stomped on a baby's head."

Grimm said: "French marigolds bring the lady bugs that eat the aphids on your tomato plants. And the aphids came here in the first place because they should have kept them Norway maples in Norway where they belong."

Grimm said: "And all them city problems started with that bussing."

Grimm said: "I read where the whole mine just flatten like a pancake."

Grimm said: "Shit."

Grimm said: "Rain stop, boy. Poosh that there."

New Years

New Year's Day

En el día más grande de mi vida, para los nenes la bendición mía, y que mis padres me den a mi bendición.

R.C.

That night a particle of me rode a gigantic horse of coal, *Noche*, with great steel hooves that left a spray of green sparks falling into the Atlantic. Clemente's plane had gone down into the troubled waters beyond San Juan. For years I galloped along the shoreline in search of him. The fishermen said now he took many shapes: a sand shark, the evening tide, a taxi driver, a woman making *pasteles* in the market, a shirt on the back of a child, even Borinquen. But I don't believe in stories, so I ran *Noche* into the ocean and we explored the reefs and floor and found the bones of stingrays and brown rum bottles and collapsed fishing boats, but never the holy wreckage, fronds of his human body.

Never.

It took me almost ten years to believe this: Roberto Clemente was dead.

First Apartment

I move away from home to be alone.

The wood beside the keyhole is gouged and scarred. Some dark thing moves in my periphery. The interior is as cozy as a fibroid uterus: pigeon feathers outside the window and across the alley the manic pulse of a woofer. Ambulance sirens are chronic like this smell of curry and garlic and cat piss. I hear popping like popcorn coming from inside a twisted garbage bag left on the fire escape. I open my box of college books and lie down on the couch to read *Burmese Days*, smoking a joint after the first paragraph. A novel about freedom, I think, at which moment a glazed cockroach the color of coffee appears on my white T-shirt. Its antennae are alert like teenaged lovers. It hesitates before the text, curious: all those vatic words scrambling to escape, little Buddhas on the great delta.

Two Grandfathers

One is a cobalt blue silhouette walking down the tracks of the Baltimore & Ohio Railroad at sunset. In his fist like a lantern, he is carrying his own severed head. The Monongahela is an ooze of molten iron spilling forward. The immigrant stops beside a boxcar to feel the breeze on his unshaved jowls and stare through his glasses at the dark foothills. While he whistles, a mother raccoon is busy searching through the dense weeds for food.

The one I never knew is reassembled through my mother's stories. He has beautiful hands. After the age of thirty, he never makes love without releasing a small ruby lizard on the walls of his bedroom. In Quito, he becomes the head of the opposition party because the poor are in love with his long, beautiful hands. Secretary General, Interior Minister, Ambassador to Chile, Mayor of Guayaquil, etcetera. In my mother's fairytale, he dies like Simón Bolívar, betrayed and poisoned by his second wife. On his deathbed, his skin turns turquoise in the coastal light and his fingernails on the white sheet are almonds of gold.

Return

Why I Return to Colombia

The enormous white clouds, the gray sky, the graphite lake, the mats of coffee drying in the sun, the two Indian women with black hats sitting in a grassy field, the alcoholic carpenter, the stone patio where the women wash clothes by hand, the silver scent of eucalyptus, the little white coffins, the German scissors, the short-wave radio playing *boleros*, the crib beside the window, the lime ovens dotting the landscape like prehistoric dwellings:

What if all the stories you knew about the past fit into tiny photographs the size of slides, black & white with crenulated borders?

Clearing Customs

Returning took thirty years: I fly into Bogotá at night.

Landing in the Andes is like a moth dipping into the side of a starry bowl.

Of all my luggage, the uniformed woman at Customs is most suspicious of my electric typewriter. I open it up for her. "What's it for?" I write poems. "What kind of poems?" Poems that shine a little flashlight into the guts of my typewriter. Poems of small children who sleep under bridges. Poems through which rivers move. Translations hawk-perched on the shoulder of a statue. Poems like lime juice falling into soup and the smell of fresh bread down every alleyway. She almost smiles; I can see only the top half of her gold tooth in the fluorescent light. Motioning me forward, "*Siga, siga,*" she says, and I pass.

A Tongue Is a Rope Bridge

I've returned to Colombia to translate (at least that's what my grant application promised). The wind is starting to kick up on the mountain path. I dictate entries for a glossary I'll never finish to the invisible woman who sits eating papaya:

Bendición = Seven days of rain, then after lunch Luzmilda's shadow on the white kitchen wall.

Manicomio = The spider walking back and forth across the ceiling, wondering which is deadlier: The seam of tiny red ants climbing up the bedpost or the mother scorpion hidden by the barred window.

Mano = The absent lover of the blue pitcher left under the flowering tree.

Camera = Wild black rabbit.

Almohada = The dream in which I listen to the motes of dust floating up like hot air balloonists over the foothills of the unmade bed.

Polillas = Your eyes, I say to the invisible woman as she tosses the peels and dark glossy seeds into the stream thirty feet below.

Madrugada = A photograph coming to life in the darkroom.

Duende = The appearance of small boys in large green hats, sometime in late afternoon. I heard from Alicia how they took the professor's son and dragged him to the place under the earth. When he returned, the skin had been stripped from his face and his clothes were in shreds.

Vicario = Reader of this page, So-and-so, with your arms at your side and a taste of pennies in your mouth.

Tunjo = A gold object found in an Indian burial mound. In other words, a prickly pear.

Estar = Where is she?

The invisible woman has long stopped writing. She's so far ahead on the turning path, all I can see in the wind with my weak eyes is the blue-green tulle of the willow.

Two Figures with Mango

Her hair in the noon sun is night-black and fine-combed and braided. The young mother sits with her baby by a wall in the south of Bogotá, peeling the speckled reddish skin deliberately in one upspiraling cut of a pocketknife. Beside her is a cart three-quarters filled with flattened cardboard boxes. She throws the peel forward toward the gutter where two pigeons peck and pull at it like the head and tail of a snake. She digs little plugs of pulp out of the orange-yellow sweet fur-soft mango and on the tip of her finger places them in the baby's mouth; he sucks and chews with his four teeth. Behind them on the wall in black spray paint:

JAIME   BATEMEN   CAYEN
Tomás Herrera e.   *En el fondo los milicos son buenos*
                        Pero en el fondo de sus TUMBAS

Villa de libertad (& in sky-blue) *Solo la lucha nos hará*
                                        LIBRES

After the Colombian Earthquake

In Pereira and Armenia rescue workers use listening devices over mounds of cement and twisted steel. Useless.

The dead are deep in thought, putting their affairs in order, remembering a kiss or the soft orange flesh of papaya. Maybe a thousand owls at midnight can hear the girl still singing in her head. Or the mute curse of the young man, God's heel crushing his spine. Now even the owls have turned away from the periodic hiss of all those little fires.

Only the ants and iridescent beetles have the courage to march into the underworld, like flute-makers and farmers going down the green mountain.

Fast Forward

Northern Wisconsin

for Janet

I'd love to put the tip of my tongue there, on that copper synapse, inside the long nape of the loon, just before she disappears.

Back Surgery and After

for Janet

My love came with whiskey and a small knife and cut me down the spine. She packed my ribs with snow and fox grape, then tied me shut with floss. The kiss on my mouth was soft as breath. Forks of rabbit and mint and orange flesh and she sang, "The wild deer of West Virginia are running on the moon, running over the gray dust of the moon." Months she laid the heavy bags of sand on me. Then like green sparks when she combs her black hair at midnight: spring came, new grass, high wind and morning rain, the hard whisper of her voice: "Walk the hollow now."

The ferns made shadows on her breast, I knelt to drink.

Fast Forward

I marry, I divorce, I put three quarters in a parking meter in Milwaukee, it's the next year, then the end of spring four years later, and now I'm married to the woman whose reflection I saw in the dark blue window of a classroom. We move to the foothills of the Alleghenies, to a farm house owned by a deaf couple. There are clouds and a blue sky, milking cows. The old man always has a hammer and a can of nails he rattles; when the windows are open you can hear him and the old woman screaming at each other. My new wife complains about the rusty water. She's thirty and urgent, I want to make a baby too, one night I mount her on the hard kitchen floor. Three weeks later her period comes heavier than the months before. By fall, still barren, we both start to see them: The blurred Amish woman in dark bonnet by the landing, the streak of the infant in her arms, the x-ray fingers of the baby, the ghost mop luminous in the corner by the starry window.

Adopting a New Life

Once upon a wheel turning through the Milky Way a woman and a man wanted something to rock and burp and change and be changed by and so they hung upside down together a good bit but alas alack and aloof with no luck to speak of. Then they spoke to the Wicken Bat who said she recommended, the man being a native of the beautiful country of Colombia, they put in an application with *Instituto Colombiano de Bienestar Familiar.* There was a lot of work and hope and worry and telephone calls and faxes and enough paper to make a sequoia but after two years they did receive a letter; it said there were two little human lives who loved to eat spaghetti, waiting for them. Here were two pictures of the wee spaghetti eaters. The man and the woman yahooed and ran to Sanso's Italian store and bought one hundred and fifty-four pounds of imported pasta and planted basil and tomato in their back yard and jumped on the back of the Wicken Bat and the next day, although momentarily the daddy thought he'd lost the key that was always in his pocket, a kind social worker in a white coat brought the couple little baby boys. One had dark eyes and the other light. The new mommy held her babies for the first time. As the daddy was signing papers and cameras were flashing, the dark-eyed baby said, "*Má.*" More.

It was his way of saying, "Time for spaghetti."

Why Given to Be Adopted

for Diego and Andrés

I once saw the face of Muhammad's Fatima in a grain of wild rice.

The human brain has more cells than the universe has stars and I imagine a crib in which a blind infant opens her eyes and listens to the *this* and *that* of crickets. You *open* your mouth and *trago* makes you swallow. Four yellow handprints on a white piece of paper is my word for *brothers*.

Your first mother at the broken window has a firefly like the stone of a ring on her longest finger and watches it go away in the night. Faith and courage.

The unknowable is a wildcat who lives at the crest of the ridge. Feel lucky if you ever see her eyes reflecting starlight toward you. Once in a playground on the spinning world I felt her soft pant on my neck.

The Hands of the Old Métis

for my father-in-law, Don Jennerjohn

One hand's arthritic and chained to the pendulum of a grandfather clock. It shakes a glass of orange juice to the trembling lips when his blood sugar falls down the stairs. Or it takes these eight pills without water and squeezes two puffs from the new inhaler.

The other, the free hand with purple bruises and dirty fingernails, strums a blond guitar in the dark front room or sharpens his pocket knife to the drum of thunder or cradles two brown ferrets and a white one. This hand works in the basement, making a small log cabin out of wood and tools and nails and glue. It places bottlecaps of water and mealworms at the bottom of the empty aquarium where the orphaned bats nest. It turns the attic globe to Canada out of boredom or pours another cup of coffee or weaves through the perfect ringlets of his new grandson.

The free hand of the electrical worker, retired eight years from Allen-Bradley, rests solid as stone on the black remote and falls asleep in the brown and orange light of the TV rodeo, at 2:00 am, his breathing machine steady as city buses through the rain.

From the Carib Word Mahiz

This is what I do: I walk through crude sunlight to the college in the former mining town, Lenni-Lenape village, place of the great forests of Pennsylvania that laid themselves down tree by tree to make the soft coal we have mostly dug and burned in the last hundred years. I walk and think of the descendants of the Maya-Quiché in Guatemala who have been retreating into the mountains for 38 years, making pale wooden crosses with writing to document their murdered aunts and uncles who have become foxes and hunting birds because if the spirits know anything it's how to survive even bulldozers and baptisms.

I walk into the classroom and open the blinds and let the sweet yellow light of this Tuesday shine on me. I smile. My new students smile back at me. It's the first day of school. There are mourning doves davening in the eaves. "Please take out a piece of paper," I say, "I want you to tell me everything you know about corn."

Augury of My Death

I ran down that street a dozen years ago half-drunk with a tall woman from Belfast I had met in a bar and we went into her apartment to get out of the rain and snort a few lines of good speed. She suggested I would find on her a rather unusual tattoo and told me about headaches she had suffered for weeks until it was discovered the old stove in the corner had leaked gas in minute quantities, and then she played a scratched recording of *La Bohème* after I said I was a poet and she confided she'd been a rope maker in Ireland before she came to this country to study the restoration of medieval texts. As we started to kiss each other's bodies like mosquitoes landing on the arms of a saint, lightning killed the lights and we took each other's clothes off on the floor and made love in the small hours on our knees and in the missionary style and at the very edge of the rough couch,until finally all we wanted to do was talk a little about chocolate and fall asleep.

In the bright morning I woke on the couch and she was lying on her belly asleep on the floor beneath me. Between her shoulder blades and running along her spine was the tattoo of an ornate I.

A vine of red and golden leaves held tiny green birds.

Earth-colored griffins stood guard in each corner.

Through a bird's eye in the center of her back I saw a dozen masked figures crowding around an open tumulus in which I was lying naked with my lips parted and ancient sunlight in my eyes.

$$\frac{64}{65}$$

Afterlife

Cellar Doors of a Small Town

One dawn every hundred years the red or gray cellar doors that open out, open up. For a few minutes, the obsessive birds are quiet, the bats' flight frozen, the morning glories anesthetized on the trellis. Over there a young black woman climbs the cellar stairs with a basket of damp clothes. On her toes she reaches up to the taut line to pin her husband's overalls. I remember the silhouette of her cotton dress edged in pink light. And on the corner of Burns and Oak, two men are hauling up the coffin of Kazbek Goutsaev who suffocated a half mile down eighty years ago in Graceton Mine No. 5. The teamster is patiently waiting, cleaning his thumbnail with a toothpick. Across the way, on Flood Street, the rusted hinges squeak; the double doors are pushed open. Someone very tall emerges, shouldering lumber, but already the features of the face and hands have begun to liquefy as the chalk-blue funnels open on the white grid and the birds start to chatter once again about technology and the banishment of solitude.

Late Supper in Northern Appalachia

Mise en scène:

The relief check is shimmed between the salt and the pepper shakers.

The mother stirs the pot of stars with a wooden spoon. The father goes whistling for the children like an ambulance in the dark. Out of the thickets they run, shirts on fire because they have been playing with matches again. One by one they march into the shower and change into fresh pajamas. The mourning dove in the bamboo cage is pecking at the air in front of her as though she sees a tiny bell. The family sits down to the brackish stew, chunks of deer meat and the isotopic glow of corn and carrots. One hand reaches for the pitcher of ice water, a smaller one for the flaky heel from the basket of bread.

Reader, they've set a place for you at the table.

"You're welcome," the mother says.

Inside the trailer, the narcotic buzzing of cicadas drowns out everything except the story you came for.

After Midnight at the Salvage Yard

How you leapt across the border of the high fence with barbed wire is still a mystery, miles and heaps of rusted steel and iron: beams, plates, axles, pipes large enough for grown men to pass through. The moon, a corroding disk, streaks down on a filthy miner, sitting, a masked coon at his feet.

His headlamp's a dim eye.

He looks at you, rubs the animal's back. "I'm sorry. Tell me if I told you before. Down at Graceton No. 5, ten minutes before the shift's up, timbers buckle, next second everything's black and here I am, or there. The woman in a white dress by the wrecking ball, with the yellow bird, do you see her yet? Sorry, that's just what I saw. Maybe you'll see something else." You turn, a doe jumping through you, seven arrows in her back.

The American Flag

Near the casino at Lac du Flambeau: no clouds, a deer skull in red leaves.

After Chaos Theory

This is the week before my mother's hysterectomy: she living with the word *cancer* inside of her, as the cocoon of fiber and blood remains inside of her, as I was once and have returned. Over my parents' house, a jet curves through darkness. Minutes pass. Then my mother says:

"On the radio they were talking about chaos theory, how the wingbeat of a butterfly on the coast of China, if nothing stopped it, could increase over time and space and completely destroy Los Angeles with wind."

Listen

Surgery's day: spring rain drips cold down the gutter to the window, beside the chimney.

It all started with a bright bleeding after Thanksgiving, wetness on a bus, she like a schoolgirl running home, washing the stained dress.

In another part of the world: a German Shepherd tied to a chain fence lets her breeder lift the hind leg and cut the artery that will spurt away from the fine coat. Her tail is wagging. She is looking back in disbelief.

I forgot to ask the surgeon with the ruby line still visible across her forehead. What will happen to my mother's uterus after the hysterectomy? After the pathologist? After housekeeping has removed in a plastic bag, tied, her pear-shaped sleeve of thick muscle?

Tonight the brick house is quiet: otherwise, only more rain, and the scraping out of ashes.

The Floating Kidney

for my mother-in-law, Betty Jennerjohn

She has a floating kidney that lectures her in Hungarian when she dreams. "*Robot, robot, robot,*" it says. It has a bad heart and a sweet tooth, water-on-the-knee and a barred owl named Gandhi who cannot fly. It's her only kidney and they're three months late with the rent. Its blood sugar is all over the place, for Christ's sake.

If the landlord calls the sheriff to evict it from its cheap apartment with the barred windows, the broken lock, the bed bugs and the music box, who will sing to it at night? Who will take it for a walk on the red leash? Who will follow its history on caterpillar treads?

After the Flood

in memory of Bill Matthews

The whole valley has been under for centuries. Only the deacon and the prothonotary had the presence of mind to die. The rest muddle through the best we can, Melinda and I making love in a bed that shifts in the silt with every thrust, the yellow dump trucks plowing water into banks of water, the letter carrier being carried away by a current to Cincinnati, clutching the leather pouch overflowing with poems past the window where I kiss Melinda on the ceiling.

Now the phone is ringing and me diving naked down the stairs to answer it. It's the other world. They ask how we are. I say: Everything isn't paradise. The lady who reads meters is bloating up like a balloon. The firemen are idle, the bars stay open all night. I don't know why or who nailed the teenager to the turning arms of the windmill. Still, when afternoon fills the arched gallery with emerald light, Melinda folding fresh linen in the basement, I make her happy by cooking, oh fish in lemon and wine.

River Spirits

When animals were no longer people, I was walking with my young sons along the river of the sliding banks. Thick plugs of wild aspargus were pushing up through the earth, and in the darkness of the forest thousands of white flowers pricked our eyes like stars. My little one was kneeling in the mulch and pine brushes, pulling back the green vertebrae of a fern. Suddenly he called out. I thought perhaps he'd found fox scat or a white spider until we crouched beside him and saw the Monongahela village.

Dwellings stretched the length of a finger, wattled walls and matted roofs. Hunters in buckskin huddled around a stone, and we could smell the gray thread of burning tobacco. A line of waterfowl was flying north over the village, not far from the orange cooking fire. Under the widest part of the fern, the older children and five women were hunkering or bent in the garden, laughing and weeding around the goosefoot, the green pumpkins, the bright sunflowers taller than the old storytelling man drinking from a gourd.

"I am finished," he said, "it is the end."

Acknowledgements

Versions of these poems have appeared in the following publications:

Clare: "The American Flag"
Ellipsis: A Journal of Literature and Art: "Behind the Stove"
Heart (Human Equity Through Art): "New Year's Day,"
    "What Appear to be Sunflowers"
Hopscotch: "El 9 de abril"
JAMA: Journal of the American Medical Association: "The Hands
    of the Old Metis," "My Love and Back Surgery"
Luna: "My Mother as a Young Woman," "Postpartum," "With
    These Scissors"
Parnassus: Poetry in Review: "Reader of This Page," "Augury of
    My Death"
Ploughshares: "Memorial Day"
Poet Lore: "My Uncle Julius"
Seneca Review: "The Floating Kidney"
The New American Poets: A Bread Loaf Anthology: "Reader of
    This Page"(reprint), "The Hands of the Old Metis" (reprint),
    "After the Colombian Earthquake," "After the Flood"

The author gratefully recognizes the careful and inspired editorial work
of Janet Carol Jennerjohn.

photo by Michele Turner

Maurice Kilwein Guevara was born in Belencito, Colombia, on the fifth of November in 1961 and raised in Pittsburgh, Pennsylvania. He was educated at the University of Pittsburgh, Bowling Green State University, and the University of Wisconsin–Milwaukee. He is Professor of English at Indiana University of Pennsylvania. He's received awards from the Bread Loaf Writers' Conference, the J. William Fulbright Commission, the Pennsylvania Council on the Arts, and the Pennsylvania Humanities Council. His first book of poetry, entitled *Postmortem* (U. of GA Press) was published in 1994. His second collection, *Poems of the River Spirit*, was published in 1996 in the Pitt Poetry Series. A dynamic presenter of his own work, Kilwein Guevara has given poetry performances in Colombia, Mexico, and throughout the United States. His work has appeared in *Poetry*, *The Kenyon Review*, *Parnassus*, *Seneca Review*, *Ploughshares*, *The Journal of the American Medical Association*, and *Exquisite Corpse*. His poetry has been anthologized in *Touching the Fire: Fifteen Poets of Today's Latino Renaissance* (Anchor/Doubleday, 1998), *American Poetry: The Next Generation* (Carnegie Mellon U. Press, 2000), and *The New American Poets: A Bread Loaf Anthology* (U. Press of New England, 2000). Recently his play, *The Last Bridge/El último puente*, was performed by the Off-Broadway production company Urban Stages. He serves on the Board of Directors of the Associated Writing Programs. He is married to Janet Jennerjohn, and they have two sons, Diego Eduardo and Andrés Esteban.

New Issues Poetry & Prose

Editor, Herbert Scott

James Armstrong, *Monument in a Summer Hat*
Michael Burkard, *Pennsylvania Collection Agency*
Anthony Butts, *Fifth Season*
Gladys Cardiff, *A Bare Unpainted Table*
Lisa Fishman, *The Deep Heart's Core Is a Suitcase*
Joseph Featherstone, *Brace's Cove*
Robert Grunst, *The Smallest Bird in North America*
Mark Halperin, *Time as Distance*
Myronn Hardy, *Approaching the Center*
Edward Haworth Hoeppner, *Rain Through High Windows*
Janet Kauffman, *Rot* (fiction)
Josie Kearns, *New Numbers*
Maurice Kilwein Guevara, *Autobiography of So-and-so:
    Poems in Prose*
Lance Larsen, *Erasable Walls*
David Dodd Lee, *Downsides of Fish Culture*
Deanne Lundin, *The Ginseng Hunter's Notebook*
Joy Manesiotis, *They Sing to Her Bones*
David Marlatt, *A Hog Slaughtering Woman*
Paula McLain, *Less of Her*
Malena Mörling, *Ocean Avenue*
Julie Moulds, *The Woman with a Cubed Head*
Marsha de la O, *Black Hope*
C. Mikal Oness, *Water Becomes Bone*
Elizabeth Powell, *The Republic of Self*
Margaret Rabb, *Granite Dives*
Rebecca Reynolds, *Daughter of the Hangnail*
Martha Rhodes, *Perfect Disappearance*
John Rybicki, *Traveling at High Speeds*
Mark Scott, *Tactile Values*
Diane Seuss-Brakeman, *It Blows You Hollow*
Marc Sheehan, *Greatest Hits*
Phillip Sterling, *Mutual Shores*
Angela Sorby, *Distance Learning*
Russell Thorburn, *Approximate Desire*
Robert VanderMolen, *Breath*
Martin Walls, *Small Human Detail in Care of National Trust*
Patricia Jabbeh Wesley, *Before the Palm Could Bloom:
    Poems of Africa*